MULTIPURPOSE ISLAMIC DUA BOOK FOR EVERY MUSLIM HOME

61 Dua's in one book

ISLAMIC DUA BOOK

by Islamic Book Store

Published by:
Islamic Book Store
302 Saad Residancy
M G Road
Bardoli
Surat, Gujarat
394601
India

Table of Contents	Page	Tick
Islamic Dua Book		
1. Dua at the time of anger	1	
2. Dua when a dog barks	1	
3. Dua when a donkey brays	1	
4. Dua when commencing anything	1	
5. When an evil thought comes to mind	2	
6. When one sees or experiences something evil	2	
7. When a fire breaks out	3	
8. After Eating	3	
9. When eating with a person who has a disease	4	
10. When clearing the dining cloth (dastarkhaan)	4	
11. Before sleeping	5	
12. Before sleeping (3)	6	
13. Dua to be read if you wake up at night	8	

Table of Contents	Page	Tick
14. Dua to be read if you wake up from a bad dream	9	
15. When seeing a Muslim laugh	10	
16. When things are in ones favour	10	
17. Dua when the sun rises	11	
18. Dua after iftaar	11	
19. When wearing new clothes	12	
20. When beginning a journey	13	
21. Dua for relief from worries and debts	15	
22. At the time of a thunderclap (1)	16	
23. At the time of a thunderclap (2)	17	
24. Dua of Hadhrat Abu Darda رضي الله عنه	18	
25. After slaughtering the Qurbaani animal	21	
26. Duas to be recited after the fardh Salaah.	22	
27. Durood to be recited on Friday after Asar	25	

Table of Contents	Page	Tick
Different forms of Durood	26	
28. When completing the Qur-aan	28	
29. Dua to be read on a hot day	30	
30. Dua to be read on a cold day	30	
31. Dua at the approach of Ramadhaan	32	
32. Dua for the month of Rajab	33	
33. Dua to be recited on the night of Baraat (Laylatul Baraat)	34	
34. Dua on Laylatul Qadr	35	
35. Dua for protection against bad manners, evil actions, evil temptations & Dreadful diseases.	35	
36. Dua When walking to the masjid	36	
37. Dua When a person comes to the door of the masjid	37	
38. Dua when a person comes out for the Fajr Salaah	38	

Table of Contents	Page	Tick
39. Dua when entering the musjid on the day of Jumuah	39	
40. Dua to be read when visiting a sick person	40	
41. Dua to be read by the sick person	41	
42. Duas to be recited before studying	43	
43. Dua for knowledge, Tolerance, Taqwa and Aafiyah	45	
44. Dua for the protection of your children from the evil eye	46	
45. Dua for protection against any harm in Buying or selling	47	
46. Dua to recite when a town/ city comes into view	48	
47. Dua to be read when any doubt occurs regarding the oneness of Allah Ta'ala	49	
48. Dua when a person has fear	50	
49. Dua When a person loses something	51	
50. Dua for the deceased	52	

Table of Contents	Page	Tick
51. Niyyah for Umrah	54	
52. Talbiyah	54	
53. On sighting the K'abah Shareef	55	
54. When drinking ZamZam water	56	
55. Some general duas.	57	
56. Masnoon duas to be recited morning & evening	60	
57. Dua for protection against harm and injury	61	
58. Morning and Evening dua	63	
59. Dua for protection from calamities	64	
60. Dua for protection on the day of Qiyaamah	66	
61. Dua for easy death	67	

1	Dua at the time of anger
2	Dua when a dog barks
3	Dua when a donkey brays

$$\text{اَعُوْذُ بِاللهِ مِنَ الشَّيْطَانِ الرَّجِيْمِ}$$

I seek the protection of Allah ﷻ from shaytaan the cursed one.

(Abu Dawood, Vol. 2, Pg. 348)

4	Dua when commencing anything

$$\text{بِسْمِ اللهِ الرَّحْمٰنِ الرَّحِيْمِ}$$

In the name of Allah ﷻ, the Most Kind, the Most Merciful.

5	When an evil thought comes to mind

اَعُوْذُ بِاللهِ مِنَ الشَّيْطَانِ الرَّجِيْمِ
اٰمَنْتُ بِاللهِ وَرُسُلِهِ

I seek the protection of Allah ﷻ from the accursed Shaitaan. I believe in Allah ﷻ and His messengers.

(MUSLIM, VOL. 1, PG. 79)

6	When one sees or experiences something evil

اَلْحَمْدُ لِلّٰهِ عَلٰى كُلِّ حَالٍ

All praise is due to Allah ﷻ under all conditions.

(IBNU MAJAH, PG. 270)

7	When a fire breaks out

$$\text{اَللّٰهُ اَكْبَرْ اَللّٰهُ اَكْبَرْ اَللّٰهُ اَكْبَرْ}$$

Allah ﷻ is the greatest. Allah ﷻ is the greatest. Allah ﷻ is the greatest. *(Tabrani {Kitaabud-Dua}, Vol. 22, Pg. 1266)*

8	After Eating

Hadhrat Abu Ayyoob A.S. reports that whenever Rasulullah [PBUH] would eat or drink, he would say:

$$\text{اَلْحَمْدُ لِلّٰهِ الَّذِیْ اَطْعَمَ وَسَقٰی وَسَوَّغَهُ وَجَعَلَ لَهُ مَخْرَجًا}$$

All praise is due to Allah ﷻ Who has given us to eat and drink, has made its entry {into our bodies} easy and has made an exit for it. *(Abu Dawood Vol. 2 Pg. 394)*

9	When eating with a person who has a disease

$$\text{بِسْمِ اللهِ ثِقَةً بِاللهِ وَتَوَكُّلًا عَلَيْهِ}$$

In the name of Allah ﷻ, with confidence in Allah ﷻ, and humbly trusting Him.

(Tirmizi, Vol. 2, Pg. 4)

10	When clearing the dining cloth (dastarkhaan)

$$\text{اَلْحَمْدُ لِلهِ حَمْدًا كَثِيْرًا طَيِّبًا مُّبَارَكًا فِيْهِ غَيْرَ مَكْفِيٍّ وَلَا مُوَدَّعٍ وَلَا مُسْتَغْنًى عَنْهُ رَبَّنَا}$$

All praise is due to Allah ﷻ, such praises which are abundant pure and filled with blessing. O our Rabb! We don't say (the food we ate) is sufficient forever nor do we bid farewell (to this food) nor are we independent of it. *(Bukhaari # 5458)*

11	Before sleeping

$$\text{اَللّٰهُمَّ قِنِيْ عَذَابَكَ يَوْمَ تَبْعَثُ عِبَادَكَ}$$

O Allah ﷻ! Save me from Your punishment on that day when You shall raise Your servants.

(Mishkaat, pg. 210)

Before sleeping (3)

بِاسْمِكَ رَبِّيْ وَضَعْتُ جَنْبِيْ وَبِكَ اَرْفَعُهُ اِنْ اَمْسَكْتَ نَفْسِيْ فَارْحَمْهَا وَاِنْ اَرْسَلْتَهَا فَاحْفَظْهَا بِمَا تَحْفَظُ بِهٖ عِبَادَكَ الصَّالِحِيْنَ

With Your name have I laid my body to rest and with Your help will I raise it. If You take my soul, do forgive it. And if You send it back, do preserve it just as You have preserved Your pious servants.

(Bukhaari Vol. 2, Pg. 935)

Note:

Nabi [PBUH] has said in a Hadith that, before going to bed, one should first dust his bed because he does not know what may be in it. Thereafter he should recite the above dua.

| 13 | Dua to be read if you wake up at night |

لَا إِلٰهَ إِلَّا اللهُ الْوَاحِدُ الْقَهَّارُ رَبُّ السَّمٰوَاتِ وَالْاَرْضِ وَمَا بَيْنَهُمَا الْعَزِيْزُ الْغَفَّارُ

There is no God but Allah ﷻ, The One, The Victorious, Rabb of the heavens and the earth and that which is between them, The all Mighty, The All forgiving.
(Nasa'I Al Kubra # 7641)

14	Dua to be read if you wake up from a bad dream

اَعُوْذُ بِكَلِمَاتِ اللهِ التَّآمَّاتِ مِنْ غَضَبِهٖ وَعِقَابِهٖ وَشَرِّ عِبَادِهٖ وَمِنْ هَمَزَاتِ الشَّيَاطِينِ وَأَنْ يَّحْضُرُوْنِ

I seek refuge in the perfect word of Allah from His anger and His punishment, from the evil of His slaves and from taunts of the shayateen and from their presence. (Tirmizi # 3528)

15	When seeing a Muslim laugh

اَضْحَكَ اللّٰهُ سِنَّكَ

May Allah ﷻ grant you lifelong happiness.

(Bukhaari, Vol, 2, Pg. 899)

16	When things are in ones favour

اَلْحَمْدُ لِلّٰهِ الَّذِىْ بِنِعْمَتِهٖ تَتِمُّ الصَّالِحَاتُ

All praise is due to Allah ﷻ with Whose grace all good things are realised.

(Ibnu Majah, PG. 270)

17	Dua when the sun rises

اَلْحَمْدُ لِلّٰهِ الَّذِىْ اَقَالَنَا يَوْمَنَا هٰذَا وَلَمْ يُهْلِكْنَا بِذُنُوْبِنَا

All praise be to Allah ﷻ, who has brought upon us this day and has not destroyed us because of our sins.
(Muslim Vol. 1, Pg. 274)

18	Dua after iftaar

ذَهَبَ الظَّمَأُ وَابْتَلَّتِ الْعُرُوْقُ وَثَبَتَ الْاَجْرُ اِنْ شَاءَ اللّٰهُ

The thirst has gone, the throat has been wetted and the reward has been earned, if Allah ﷻ so wills.
(Abu Dawood Vol. 1, Pg. 328)

19	When wearing new clothes

اَلْحَمْدُ لِلّٰهِ الَّذِيْ كَسَانِيْ مَا اُوَارِيْ بِهٖ عَوْرَتِيْ وَاَتَجَمَّلُ بِهٖ فِيْ حَيَاتِيْ

Praise be to Allah ﷻ, who clothed me with that which I cover my shame and adorn myself with during my life.
(Tirmizi, Vol. 2, Pg. 195)

Virtue

It is mentioned in the Hadith that if a person recites this dua after wearing new clothes and he gives his old clothes in sadaqah (charity), then he will be in the guardianship and protection of Allah ﷻ.   *(Tirmizi, Vol. 2, Pg. 195)*

When beginning a journey

اَللهُ اَكْبَرُ اَللهُ اَكْبَرُ اَللهُ اَكْبَرُ اَللّٰهُمَّ اِنَّا نَسْأَلُكَ فِيْ سَفَرِنَا هٰذَا الْبِرَّ وَالتَّقْوٰى وَمِنَ الْعَمَلِ مَا تَرْضٰى اَللّٰهُمَّ هَوِّنْ عَلَيْنَا سَفَرَنَا هٰذَا وَاطْوِ عَنَّا بُعْدَهُ اَللّٰهُمَّ اَنْتَ الصَّاحِبُ فِي السَّفَرِ وَالْخَلِيْفَةُ فِي الْاَهْلِ. اَللّٰهُمَّ اِنِّيْ اَعُوْذُ بِكَ مِنْ وَّعْثَآءِ السَّفَرِ وَكَآبَةِ الْمَنْظَرِ وَسُوْٓءِ الْمُنْقَلَبِ فِي الْمَالِ وَالْاَهْلِ وَالْوَلَدِ

Allah ﷻ is the Greatest! Allah ﷻ is the Greatest! Allah ﷻ is the Greatest! O Allah ﷻ, we ask You to grant us, in this journey of ours, piety, abstinence (from sin) and the ability to do actions that are pleasing to You. O Allah ﷻ, make easy for us this journey and shorten for us its destination. O Allah ﷻ, You are our Companion on this journey and the Protector of our families. O Allah ﷻ, I seek Your protection against the hardships of this journey, against a bad scene and against making a bad return to my belongings, wife and children. *(Muslim, Vol. 1, Pg. 434)*

Sunnats of travelling

1. Recite all the masnoon duas of travelling.
2. Read two rakaats nafl salaah before the journey.
3. Inform your family about your whereabouts.
4. Keep necessary personal information on yourself, or whatever documents one may require on his journey. (e.g. passport, I.D. etc.)
5. Be punctual with all your salaah whilst on your journey.
6. Do not inconvenience anyone whilst on journey.

| 21 | Dua for relief from worries and debts |

اَللّٰهُمَّ اِنِّيْ اَعُوْذُ بِكَ مِنَ الْهَمِّ وَالْحُزْنِ وَاَعُوْذُ بِكَ مِنَ الْعَجْزِ وَالْكَسْلِ وَاَعُوْذُ بِكَ مِنَ الْجُبْنِ وَالْبُخْلِ وَاَعُوْذُ بِكَ مِنْ غَلَبَةِ الدَّيْنِ وَقَهْرِ الرِّجَالِ

O Allah! I seek Your protection from worry and grief, and I seek Your protection from weakness and laziness, and I seek Your protection from miserliness and cowardice and I seek Your protection from the burden of debt and the anger of men.

(Abu Dawood, Vol. 1 Pg. 224)

22	At the time of a thunderclap (1)

اَللّٰهُمَّ لَا تَقْتُلْنَا بِغَضَبِكَ وَلَا تُهْلِكْنَا بِعَذَابِكَ وَعَافِنَا قَبْلَ ذَالِكَ

O Allah, do not kill us through Your anger and do not destroy us with Your punishment. Do forgive us before this (happens). *(Tirmizi, Vol. 2, Pg. 183)*

| 23 | At the time of a thunderclap (2) |

$$\text{سُبْحَانَ الَّذِي يُسَبِّحُ الرَّعْدُ بِحَمْدِهِ وَالْمَلَائِكَةُ مِنْ خِيفَتِهِ}$$

Glory be to Allah ﷾, The Being whom thunder as well as the Angels praise and glorify Him out of fear for Him.

(Muatta Imaam Maalik # 3641)

24 — Dua of Hadhrat Abu Darda رضي الله عنه

اَللّٰهُمَّ اَنْتَ رَبِّيْ لَاۤ اِلٰهَ اِلَّاۤ اَنْتَ عَلَيْكَ تَوَكَّلْتُ وَاَنْتَ رَبُّ الْعَرْشِ الْعَظِيْمِ. مَاشَآءَ اللهُ كَانَ وَمَا لَمْ يَشَأْ لَمْ يَكُنْ لَا حَوْلَ وَلَاقُوَّةَ اِلَّا بِاللهِ الْعَلِيِّ الْعَظِيْمِ. اَعْلَمُ اَنَّ اللهَ عَلٰى كُلِّ شَيْءٍ قَدِيْرٌ. وَاَنَّ اللهَ قَدْ اَحَاطَ بِكُلِّ شَيْءٍ عِلْمًا. اَللّٰهُمَّ اِنِّيْ اَعُوْذُ بِكَ مِنْ شَرِّ نَفْسِيْ وَمِنْ شَرِّ كُلِّ دَآبَّةٍ اَنْتَ اٰخِذٌ بِنَاصِيَتِهَا اِنَّ رَبِّيْ عَلٰى صِرَاطٍ مُّسْتَقِيْمٍ

O Allah سُبْحَانَهُوَتَعَالَىٰ! You are my Rabb, other than You there is no God. It is upon You that I have faith and You are the Rabb of the Mighty Throne. Whatever Allah سُبْحَانَهُوَتَعَالَىٰ has wished has happened and whatever He has not wished will certainly not happen. Without the assistance of Allah سُبْحَانَهُوَتَعَالَىٰ, we cannot save ourselves from any evil nor can we acquire any good. I am sure that Allah سُبْحَانَهُوَتَعَالَىٰ has power over everything and verily the knowledge of Allah سُبْحَانَهُوَتَعَالَىٰ encompasses everything.

O Allah سُبْحَانَهُوَتَعَالَىٰ I seek refuge in You from the evil of myself and the evil of all the living upon whom You have control. Verily, my Rabb is on the right path.

Virtue

Someone came and informed Hadhrat Abu Darda رَضِيَ اللهُ عَنْهُ that his house was on fire. Hadhrat Abu Darda رَضِيَ اللهُ عَنْهُ [without any concern] replied that his house was certainly not on fire. Allah سُبْحَانَهُ وَتَعَالَى will never do so, because I have heard from Rasulullah صَلَّى اللهُ عَلَيْهِ وَسَلَّمَ that if a person recites these words at the beginning of the day, no calamities will befall that person till the evening, and if the person recites these words in the evening then no calamities will befall that person till the morning.

In another narration, it is stated that calamities will not befall him, his wife, children and whatever he owns.

Hadhrat Abu Darda رَضِيَ اللهُ عَنْهُ said: "In the morning I recited these words, therefore, how can my house be on fire." He then said to the people. "Let's go and see." Together with the people they went towards his house. It was seen that his entire street was on fire and all the houses around Hadhrat Abu Darda's رَضِيَ اللهُ عَنْهُ were burnt, but, amidst this, his house was safe and sound.

(Al-Azkaar-Nawawi, Pg. 79)

| 25 | After slaughtering the Qurbaani animal |

اَللّٰهُمَّ تَقَبَّلْهُ مِنِّىْ كَمَا تَقَبَّلْتَ مِنْ حَبِيْبِكَ مُحَمَّدٍ صَلَّى اللهُ عَلَيْهِ وَسَلَّمَ وَخَلِيْلِكَ اِبْرَاهِيْمَ عَلَيْهِمَا الصَّلَاةُ وَالسَّلَامُ

O Allah!, accept it (this sacrifice) from me just as You have accepted from Your Beloved Muhammad [PBUH] and Your Close Friend Ibraheem A.S.

(Baheshti Zewar Pg.231)

| 26 | Duas to be recited after the fardh Salaah. |

اَللهُ اَكْبَرُ اَسْتَغْفِرُ اللهَ ، اَسْتَغْفِرُ اللهَ ، اَسْتَغْفِرُ اللهَ

Allah Ta'ala is the greatest I beg Allah ﷻ for forgiveness.

اَللّٰهُمَّ اَنْتَ السَّلَامُ وَمِنْكَ السَّلَامُ تَبَارَكْتَ يَاذَا الْجَلَالِ وَالْاِكْرَامِ

O Allah you are peace and from you comes peace. Blessed are You; O the one of Supreme Greatness, beholder of absolute independence; who exceeds in nobleness and courtesy. (Muslim # 136)

اَللّٰهُمَّ اَعِنِّيْ عَلٰى ذِكْرِكَ وَشُكْرِكَ وَحُسْنِ عِبَادَتِكَ

O Allah help me in remembering You and in thanking You and worshiping You in the best manner.

(Abu Dawood)

رَبَّنَآ اٰتِنَا فِي الدُّنْيَا حَسَنَةً وَّفِي الْاٰخِرَةِ حَسَنَةً وَّقِنَا عَذَابَ النَّارِ

O Allah, grant us the good of this world and the good of the Hereafter and save us from the punishment of the fire.

اَللّٰهُمَّ لَا مَانِعَ لِمَا اَعْطَيْتَ وَلَا مُعْطِيَ لِمَا مَنَعْتَ وَلَا رَآدَّ لِمَا قَضَيْتَ وَلَا يَنْفَعُ ذَا الْجَدِّ مِنْكَ الْجَدُّ

O Allah None can prevent what You bestow and none can bestow what You prevent. None can reverse what You decreed and the wealth of the wealthy in front of You (O Allah) is of no benefit to them. [Muslim # 477]

| 27 | Durood to be recited on Friday after Asar |

اَللّٰهُمَّ صَلِّ عَلٰى سَيِّدِنَا مُحَمَّدٍ النَّبِيِّ الْاُمِّيِّ وَعَلٰى اٰلِهٖ وَسَلِّمْ تَسْلِيْمًا

O Allah! Shower special mercy and great peace upon our master Muhammad [PBUH] the unlettered nabi and upon his family.

Virtue

Abu Hurairah ﷺ says that Nabi ﷺ said, "Whosoever remained seated after Asr Salaah on a Friday, and before rising from his seating place recites eighty times the above Durood then his sins of eighty years are forgiven and the reward for the ibaadah for eighty years are written for him."

Different forms of Durood

اَللّٰهُمَّ صَلِّ عَلٰى مُحَمَّدٍ كُلَّمَا ذَكَرَهُ الذَّاكِرُوْنَ وَصَلِّ عَلٰى مُحَمَّدٍ كُلَّمَا غَفَلَ عَنْ ذِكْرِهِ الْغَافِلُوْنَ

O Allah! Bestow mercy upon Muhammad [PBUH] as numerous as the number of times as those who remember him and bestow mercy upon Muhammad [PBUH] as numerous as the number of times as those who neglect to remember him.

Bdy'a

Virtue

Imaam Shafiee mentioned to someone in a dream after he passed away, "Allah Ta'ala forgave me and ordered that I be taken to Jannah with great honour and dignity. This was all in reward for reciting this durood."

اَللّٰهُمَّ صَلِّ عَلٰى مُحَمَّدٍ عَبْدِكَ وَرَسُوْلِكَ وَصَلِّ عَلَى الْمُؤْمِنِيْنَ وَالْمُؤْمِنَاتِ وَالْمُسْلِمِيْنَ وَالْمُسْلِمَاتِ

O Allah, send salaat on Muhammad [PBUH], Your servant and Your messenger and send salaat on all the Mu'min (believing) males and females and the Muslim males and females.

جَزَى اللهُ عَنَّا نَبِيَّنَا مُحَمَّدًا صَلَّى اللهُ عَلَيْهِ وَسَلَّمَ بِمَا هُوَ اَهْلُهٗ

O Allah! grant our Noble Master Muhammad [PBHU] a suitable reward on our behalf.

Kanzul Ummaal # 3900

When completing the Qur-aan

اَللّٰهُمَّ اٰنِسْ وَحْشَتِىْ فِىْ قَبْرِىْ اَللّٰهُمَّ ارْحَمْنِىْ بِالْقُرْاٰنِ الْعَظِيْمِ وَاجْعَلْهُ لِىْ اِمَامًا وَّنُوْرًا وَّهُدًى وَّرَحْمَةً. اَللّٰهُمَّ ذَكِّرْنِىْ مِنْهُ مَا نَسِيْتُ وَعَلِّمْنِىْ مِنْهُ مَا جَهِلْتُ وَارْزُقْنِىْ تِلَاوَتَهٗ اٰنَآءَ اللَّيْلِ وَاٰنَآءَ النَّهَارِ وَاجْعَلْهُ لِىْ حُجَّةً يَّارَبَّ الْعَالَمِيْنَ

O Allah! divert my restlessness in the grave into peace. O Allah let me receive Your mercy by means of the Holy Qur-aan Shareef and make it my guide as well as a source of light, guidance and grace for me. O Allah, revive my memory of whatever I have forgotten from the Holy Qur-aan, grant me understanding of whatever part of it I know not, enable me to recite it during hours of the day and the night and make it my main argumentative support (in all matters), O Nourisher of the worlds.

(Al-Mughni an mahal lil asfaar lil Iraaqi Vol. 1, Pg. 279 -It-haaf Vol. 4, Pg. 496)

29 — Dua to be read on a hot day

لَا إِلٰهَ إِلَّا اللّٰهُ مَا أَشَدَّ حَرَّ هٰذَا الْيَوْمِ
اَللّٰهُمَّ اَجِرْنِيْ مِنْ حَرِّ جَهَنَّمَ

There is no God besides Allah ﷾ How severe is the heat of this day. O' Allah save me from the heat of Jahannam.

(Amal-ul-yaum-wal-laylah Ibne Sunni (R.A)

30 — Dua to be read on a cold day

لَا إِلٰهَ إِلَّا اللّٰهُ مَا أَشَدَّ بَرْدَ هٰذَا الْيَوْمِ
اَللّٰهُمَّ اَجِرْنِيْ مِنْ زَمْهَرِيْرِ جَهَنَّمَ

There is no God besides Allah ﷾ how severe is the cold of this day. O' Allah save me from the cold of Jahannam.

(Amal-ul-yaum-wal-laylah Ibne Sunni (R.A)

The cold weather of winter should remind one of the 'severe cold' of Jahannam. Sayyiduna ibn Abbaas R.A says, 'The inmates of Jahannam will ask to be rescued from the excruciating heat of Jahannam. An icy cold wind will be blown upon them, which will cause their bones to ache after which they will beg for heat again.'

Rasulullah [PBUH] is reported to have said, 'When a person recites the above duas, Allah سُبْحَانَهُ وَتَعَالَى says to Jahannam, 'Indeed, a servant of mine has sought refuge in me from you, bear testimony that I have granted him salvation from you.'

| 31 | Dua at the approach of Ramadhaan |

اَللّٰهُمَّ سَلِّمْنِيْ لِرَمَضَانَ وَسَلِّمْ رَمَضَانَ لِيْ وَسَلِّمْهُ لِيْ مُتَقَبَّلاً

O Allah! Safeguard me for the Month of Ramadhaan (by making me see the Month of Ramadhaan healthy and fit so that I can take maximum benefit from it), and safeguard the Month of Ramadhaan for me (by making the conditions in it such that I can take maximum benefit from it) and accept it from me.

(Kanz-ul-ummal, Vol.8, Pg. 584 Hadith 24277)

Dua for the month of Rajab

$$\text{اَللّٰهُمَّ بَارِكْ لَنَا فِىْ رَجَبٍ وَّشَعْبَانَ وَبَلِّغْنَا رَمَضَانَ}$$

Hadhrat Anas R.A. reports that whenever the month of Rajab would arrive, Rasulullah [PBUH] would make the following dua, "O Allah! Bless us in the months of Rajab and Sha'baan and allow us to witness the month of Ramadhaan."

33	Dua to be recited on the night of Baraat (Laylatul Baraat)

It is reported in a Hadith that Rasulullah [PBHU] said to Hadhrat 'Aaisha رَضِيَ اللهُ عَنْهَا: "On this night (Shabe Baraat) read this dua and teach it to others. Jibra'eel عَلَيْهِ السَّلَامُ taught this dua to me."

اَعُوْذُ بِعَفْوِكَ مِنْ عِقَابِكَ وَاَعُوْذُ بِرِضَاكَ
مِنْ سَخَطِكَ وَاَعُوْذُ بِكَ مِنْكَ جَلَّ وَجْهُكَ
لَااُحْصِىْ ثَنَاءً عَلَيْكَ اَنْتَ كَمَا اَثْنَيْتَ عَلٰى
نَفْسِكَ

I seek protection in Your forgiveness from Your punishment; and I seek shelter in Your pleasure from Your displeasure; and I seek safety in You, from You. Glory be to You. I am unable to fully praise you. You are as You have praised yourself. (O My Rabb).

34	Dua on Laylatul Qadr

$$\text{اَللّٰهُمَّ اِنَّكَ عَفُوٌّ تُحِبُّ الْعَفْوَ فَاعْفُ عَنِّيْ}$$

O Allah! Verily You are most forgiving, You love to forgive, so please forgive me. (Ibn-e-Maajh #3850)

35	Dua for protection against bad manners, evil actions, evil temptations & Dreadful diseases.

$$\text{اَللّٰهُمَّ اِنِّيْ اَعُوْذُ بِكَ مِنْ مُنْكَرَاتِ الْاَخْلَاقِ وَالْاَعْمَالِ وَالْاَهْوَاءِ وَالْاَدْوَاءِ}$$

O Allah, I seek Your Protection from Bad manners, evil actions, evil temptations and dreadful diseases.

(Kanzul Umaal Vol. 2 Pg 277)

Dua When walking to the masjid

اَللّٰهُمَّ اِنِّیْ اَسْئَلُكَ بِحَقِّ السَّآئِلِیْنَ عَلَیْكَ وَبِحَقِّ مَمْشَایَ هٰذَا فَاِنِّیْ لَمْ اَخْرُجْ اَشَرًا وَّلَا بَطَرًا وَّلَا رِیَآءً وَّلَا سُمْعَةً خَرَجْتُ اِتِّقَآءَ سَخْطِكَ وَابْتِغَآءَ مَرْضَاتِكَ اَسْئَلُكَ اَنْ تُنْقِذَنِیْ مِنَ النَّارِ وَاَنْ تَغْفِرَ لِیْ ذُنُوْبِیْ اِنَّهُ لَا یَغْفِرُ الذُّنُوْبَ اِلَّا اَنْتَ

O Allah! Through the blessings of those who ask of You and through this coming out of mine for I have not come out in arrogance nor in pride nor in show nor in fame. Rather I came out fearing Your displeasure and seeking Your pleasure. I beg of You that You save me from the fire (of Jahannam) and that You forgive my sins for verily none but You forgives sins.

It is mentioned in a Hadith that whomsoever recites this dua when walking towards the Masjid, Allah Ta'ala appoints 70 000 Malaaikah to seek forgiveness on his behalf and Allah Ta'ala places His special *tawajjuh* (focus) on him until he completes his salaah. [Musnad Ahmad #11172]

37	Dua When a person comes to the door of the masjid

O Allah! I seek protection from Iblees and his armies.
(Amal-ul-yaum-wal-laylah Ibne Sunni # 154)

38	Dua when a person comes out for the Fajr Salaah

اَللّٰهُمَّ اجْعَلْ فِيْ قَلْبِيْ نُوْرًا وَّاجْعَلْ فِيْ لِسَانِيْ نُوْرًا وَّاجْعَلْ فِيْ سَمْعِيْ نُوْرًا وَّاجْعَلْ فِيْ بَصَرِيْ نُوْرًا وَّاجْعَلْ مِنْ خَلْفِيْ نُوْرًا وَّمِنْ اَمَامِيْ نُوْرًا وَّاجْعَلْ مِنْ فَوْقِيْ نُوْرًا وَّمِنْ تَحْتِيْ نُوْرًا اَللّٰهُمَّ وَاَعْظِمْ لِيْ نُوْرًا

O Allah, fill Your noor (light) into my heart, my tongue, my ears, my eyes, behind me, in front of me, over me and beneath me, O Allah, bestow me with Your (Noor) light

(Abu Dawood Vol 1 Pg. 515)

39	Dua when entering the musjid on the day of Jumuah

اَللّٰهُمَّ اجْعَلْنِيْ اَوْجَهَ مَنْ تَوَجَّهَ اِلَيْكَ وَاَقْرَبَ مَنْ تَقَرَّبَ اِلَيْكَ وَاَفْضَلَ مَنْ سَاَلَكَ وَرَغِبَ اِلَيْكَ

O Allah! Make me the most focused person towards You and the closest of those who attempted to come close to You and make me the most blessed of those who ask of You and are yearning for You.

(Amal-ul-yaum-wal-laylah Ibne Sunni (R.A), Pg. 211)

40	Dua to be read when visiting a sick person

Reciting the following *du'a* seven times near the sick person is extremely beneficial.

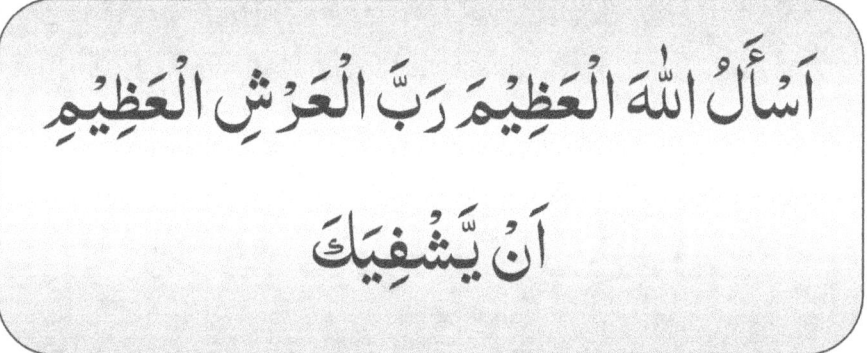

I Beseech Allah ﷻ the Great, the Rabb of the Great Throne, to cure you.

(Abu Dawood # 3108)

> ### Virtue
>
> It is mentioned in a Hadith that whosoever recites the above *du'a* seven times near a sick person, he will definitely be cured, provided he is not in his terminal illness. (Amalul yomi pg. 301)
>
> Whenever Hadhrat Ibn-Umar رضى الله عنه went to visit a sick person he enquired about his health, and when he stood up to leave, he made the following *du'a*

41	Dua to be read by the sick person

In another Hadith it is narrated that any sick Muslim who recites the following dua forty times and thereafter passes away, receives the reward of a *shaheed* and, if he is cured, then all his sins will be

> لَا اِلٰهَ اِلَّا اَنْتَ سُبْحَانَكَ اِنِّىْ كُنْتُ مِنَ الظَّالِمِيْنَ

There is no deity besides Allah سبحانه وتعالى; He is free from all blemishes; verily I am one of the sinners

(Hisne Haseen, Pg, 177)

In one Hadith it is mentioned that, when you visit a sick person, place your right hand on his body (i.e. his head or the place of pain) and read the following dua:

اَذْهِبِ الْبَأْسَ رَبَّ النَّاسِ اِشْفِ اَنْتَ الشَّافِىْ لَا شِفَاءَ اِلَّا شِفَاءَكَ شِفَاءً لَّا يُغَادِرُ سَقَمًا

O Allah! Remove this sickness. O Rabb of humanity, grant cure, for only You are the curer. Indeed, cure is only from You. Grant such cure after which no sickness will follow. (Hisne Haseen, Pg. 176)

42	Duas to be recited before studying

It was the general practice of our pious and saintly learned Ulama to recite the under mentioned *aayaat* and *du'as* when commencing to teach.

Before learning we should also recite the following duas.

سُبْحَانَكَ لَا عِلْمَ لَنَآ اِلَّا مَا عَلَّمْتَنَآ اِنَّكَ اَنْتَ الْعَلِيْمُ الْحَكِيْمُ

O Allah You are most certainly pure of all faults; for indeed there is no (favour of Deeni) knowledge for us accept that which You have allowed us to learn, surely You are All Knowing, Most Wise.

> رَبِّ اشْرَحْ لِي صَدْرِي وَيَسِّرْ لِي أَمْرِي وَاحْلُلْ عُقْدَةً مِّن لِّسَانِي يَفْقَهُوا قَوْلِي

O my Sustainer, open my chest (to Your enlightment), and make easy for me my task (in this regard), and open the knot (of stuttering) in my tongue, so that the people may understand my message.

> رَبِّ زِدْنِي عِلْمًا

رَبِّ يَسِّرْ وَلَا تُعَسِّرْ وَتَمِّمْ بِالْخَيْرِ وَبِكَ نَسْتَعِيْنُ يَا فَتَّاحُ

O my Sustainer, make this (task of acquiring Deeni Ilm) easy for me, and do not cause any difficulty for me therein. Allow me to complete it with all goodness and grace. O the One who made clear the path between truth and falsehood and is all knowing, and indeed from You alone do we seek assistance.

43	Dua for knowledge, Tolerance, Taqwa and Aafiyah

اَللّٰهُمَّ اَغْنِنِيْ بِالْعِلْمِ وَزَيِّنِّيْ بِالْحِلْمِ وَاَكْرِمْنِيْ بِالتَّقْوٰى وَجَمِّلْنِيْ بِالْعَافِيَةِ

O Allah endow me with knowledge, beautify me with tolerance, honour me with *taqwa* (fear of Allah) and beautify me with *Aafiyah* (good conditions). _(Kanz-ul-ummal # 3663)

44	Dua for the protection of your children from the evil eye

أَعُوْذُ بِكَلِمَاتِ اللهِ التَّآمَّةِ مِنْ كُلِّ شَيْطَانٍ وَهَآمَّةٍ وَمِنْ كُلِّ عَيْنٍ لَّامَّةٍ

I seek refuge in the perfect Words of Allah ﷻ from every shaytaan and harmful creature, and from every evil eye. *(Bukhaari # 3371)*

45	Dua for protection against any harm in Buying or selling

بِسْمِ اللهِ اَللّٰهُمَّ اِنِّىْ اَسْئَالُكَ مِنْ خَيْرِ هٰذِهِ السُّوْقِ وَخَيْرِ مَا فِيْهَا وَاَعُوْذُبِكَ مِنْ شَرِّ هٰذِهِ السُّوْقِ وَشَرِّ مَا فِيْهَا وَاَعُوْذُبِكَ اَنْ اُصِيْبَ فِيْهَا يَمِيْنًا فَاجِرَةً اَوْ صَفْقَةً خَاسِرَةً

O Allah! I ask You for the good of this bazaar and the good therein and I seek protection in You from the evil of this bazaar and the evil herein and I seek protection in You from taking a sinful oath in here or incurring a business loss.

(Hisne Haseen, Pg. 428)

46	Dua to recite when a town/ city comes into view

اَللّٰهُمَّ رَبَّ السَّمَاوَاتِ السَّبْعِ وَمَا اَظْلَلْنَ وَرَبَّ الْاَرْضِيْنَ السَّبْعِ وَمَا اَقْلَلْنَ وَرَبَّ الشَّيَاطِيْنِ وَمَا اَضْلَلْنَ وَرَبَّ الرِّيَاحِ وَمَا ذَرَيْنَ فَاِنَّا نَسْئَلُكَ خَيْرَ هٰذِهِ الْقَرْيَةِ وَخَيْرَ اَهْلِهَا وَنَعُوْذُبِكَ مِنْ شَرِّهَا وَشَرِّ اَهْلِهَا وَشَرِّ مَا فِيْهَا

O Allah! Rabb of the seven heavens and what they overshadowed, Rabb of the seven earths and what they bear, Rabb of the shayateen and whosoever they have misled, Rabb of the winds and what they have blown. We beg of You the goodness of this settlement and its inhabitants and we seek Your protection from the evils of this settlement and its inhabitants and from what evil is contained therein.

(Mustadrak Hakim, V.1, P.446)

| 47 | Dua to be read when any doubt occurs regarding the oneness of Allah Ta'ala |

اَللّٰهُ اَحَدٌ اَللّٰهُ الصَّمَدُ لَمْ يَلِدْ وَلَمْ يُوْلَدْ وَلَمْ يَكُنْ لَّهٗ كُفُوًا اَحَدٌ

Allah Ta'ala is most independent, He did not beget nor was He begotten and no one is equal to Him.

(Ma'rijul Qubool Vol.1, Pg.195)

| 48 | Dua when a person has fear |

سُبْحَانَ الْمَلِكِ الْقُدُّوْسِ رَبُّ الْمَلَئِكَةِ وَالرُّوْحِ جُلِّلَتِ السَّمٰوٰتُ وَالْاَرْضُ بِالْعِزَّةِ وَالْجَبَرُوْتِ

Most pure is the exalted king, The Rabb of the malaaikah and Jibreel A.S. The skies and the earth are enveloped in the power and might of Allah Ta'ala.

(Al M'uajamul Kabeer Vol 2 Pg. 24)

| 49 | Dua When a person loses something |

اَللّٰهُمَّ رَآدَّ الضَّآلَّةِ وَهَادِيَ الضَّالَةِ تَهْدِىْ مِنَ الضَّلَالَةِ اُرْدُدْ عَلَىَّ ضَآلَّتِىْ بِقُدْرَتِكَ وَسُلْطَانِكَ فَاِنَّهَا مِنْ عَطَآئِكَ وَفَضْلِكَ

O Allah! The One who returns back the lost and the One who guides back the lost, You are the One who guides back the astray through Your power and might return to me my lost item for verily it is that which You granted and from Your grace. (Majmauz Zawaaid # 17106)

Dua for the deceased

اَللّٰهُمَّ اغْفِرْ لَهُ وَارْحَمْهُ وَعَافِهِ وَاعْفُ عَنْهُ وَاَكْرِمْ نُزُلَهُ وَوَسِّعْ مَدْخَلَهُ وَاغْسِلْهُ بِالْمَآءِ وَالثَّلْجِ وَالْبَرَدِ وَنَقِّهِ مِنَ الْخَطَايَا كَمَا يُنَقَّى الثَّوْبُ الْاَبْيَضُ مِنَ الدَّنَسِ وَاَبْدِلْهُ دَارًا خَيْرًا مِّنْ دَارِهِ وَاَهْلًا خَيْرًا مِّنْ اَهْلِهِ وَزَوْجًا خَيْرًا مِّنْ زَوْجِهِ وَاَدْخِلْهُ الْجَنَّةَ وَاَعِذْهُ مِنْ عَذَابِ الْقَبْرِ وَمِنْ عَذَابِ النَّارِ

O Allah! Forgive him. Have mercy upon him. Give him peace and absolve him. Receive him honourably, and make his grave spacious. Wash him with the water, snow and hail. Cleanse him from faults as You cleanse a white garment from impurity.

Replace him with an abode better than his abode, with a household better than his household. Admit him to Jannat and protect him from the torment of the grave and punishment of the Fire. (Musnadul Bazar Vol. 7 Pg 172)

| 51 | Niyyah for Umrah |

$$\text{اَللّٰهُمَّ اِنِّىْ اُرِيْدُ الْعُمْرَةَ فَيَسِّرْهَا لِىْ وَتَقَبَّلْهَا مِنِّىْ}$$

O Allah! I intend performing umrah. Thus render it easy for, me and accept it from me. (Maraaqi Ul Falaah Vol. 1 Pg

| 52 | Talbiyah |

$$\text{لَبَّيْكَ اَللّٰهُمَّ لَبَّيْكَ لَبَّيْكَ لَا شَرِيْكَ لَكَ لَبَّيْكَ اِنَّ الْحَمْدَ وَالنِّعْمَةَ لَكَ وَالْمُلْكَ لَا شَرِيْكَ لَكَ}$$

Here I am at your service O Allah! I am present, I am present, You have no partner, all praise and graciousness as well as the entire universe is Yours, You have no partner.

| 53 | On sighting the K'abah Shareef |

اَللّٰهُمَّ اَنْتَ السَّلَامُ وَمِنْكَ السَّلَامُ فَحَيِّنَا رَبَّنَا بِالسَّلَامِ اَللّٰهُمَّ زِدْ بَيْتَكَ هٰذَا تَعْظِيْمًا وَّتَشْرِيْفًا وَّتَكْرِيْمًا وَّمَهَابَةً وَزِدْ مِنْ شَرَفِهِ وَعِظَمِهِ وَكَرَمِهِ مِمَّنْ حَجَّهُ اَوِ اعْتَمَرَهْ تَشْرِيْفًا وَّتَعْظِيْمًا وَّبِرًّا

O Allah! You are full of peace, and from You is peace, therefore keep us alive with peace. O Allah! Increase this house of Yours with reverence, dignity, honour and respect, and increase those who perform haj or umrah towards it in dignity, honour, reverence, obedience and righteousness. (Tabyeenul Haqaaiq Vol. 2 Pg 15)

54	When drinking ZamZam water

$$\text{اَللّٰهُمَّ اِنِّیْ اَسْاَلُكَ عِلْمًا نَّافِعًا وَّرِزْقًا وَّاسِعًا وَّشِفَآءً مِّنْ كُلِّ دَاءٍ}$$

O Allah ! I am asking you for beneficial knowledge, and abundance in provision, and cure from every ailment. (Durul Manthur Vol. 7 Pg. 284)

55 — Some general duas.

رَبَّنَا لَا تُؤَاخِذْنَا إِنْ نَسِينَا أَوْ أَخْطَأْنَا رَبَّنَا وَلَا تَحْمِلْ عَلَيْنَا إِصْرًا كَمَا حَمَلْتَهُ عَلَى الَّذِينَ مِنْ قَبْلِنَا رَبَّنَا وَلَا تُحَمِّلْنَا مَا لَا طَاقَةَ لَنَا بِهِ وَاعْفُ عَنَّا وَاغْفِرْ لَنَا وَارْحَمْنَا أَنْتَ مَوْلَانَا فَانْصُرْنَا عَلَى الْقَوْمِ الْكَافِرِينَ

"O Allah! Do not punish us if we forget or fall into error; O Allah! Do not burden us like how You did on those before us; O Allah! Do not burden us with something greater than we have strength to bear. Forgive our sins, and grant us Forgiveness. Have Mercy on us. You are Our Protector; help us against the kuffaar."

رَبَّنَآ ءَاتِنَا فِي الدُّنْيَا حَسَنَةً وَّفِي الْأَخِرَةِ حَسَنَةً وَّقِنَا عَذَابَ النَّارِ

"O Allah! Give us good in this world and good in the Hereafter, and save us from the punishment of the Fire!"

رَبَّنَا ظَلَمْنَآ أَنْفُسَنَا وَإِنْ لَّمْ تَغْفِرْ لَنَا وَتَرْحَمْنَا لَنَكُونَنَّ مِنَ الْخَاسِرِينَ

"O Allah! we have wronged Our souls: If You do not forgive us and have mercy on us, we shall certainly be lost."

رَبَّنَا لَا تُزِغْ قُلُوبَنَا بَعْدَ إِذْ هَدَيْتَنَا وَهَبْ لَنَا مِن لَّدُنكَ رَحْمَةً إِنَّكَ أَنتَ الْوَهَّابُ

O Allah! do not let our hearts deviate after You have guided us, but grant us Your Mercy; for verily You are the Grantor of bounties without measure.

سُبْحَانَ رَبِّكَ رَبِّ الْعِزَّةِ عَمَّا يَصِفُونَ، وَسَلَامٌ عَلَى الْمُرْسَلِينَ، وَالْحَمْدُ لِلَّهِ رَبِّ الْعَالَمِينَ

Your Rabb, The Rabb of all honour is pure (free) from what (partners and children) they attribute to Him. Peace be upon the ambiyaa. And all praise belongs to Allah Ta'ala, the Rabb of the universe.

56	Masnoon duas to be recited morning & evening

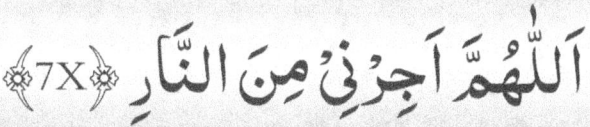

O Allah save us from the punishment of Jahannam.

(Abu Dawood, Vol.2, Pg. 345)

I seek the protection of the Absolute Words of Allah from the evil He has created.

57	Dua for protection against harm and injury

Recite three times morning and evening

بِسْمِ اللهِ الَّذِىْ لَا يَضُرُّ مَعَ اسْمِهٖ شَىْءٌ فِى الْاَرْضِ وَلَا فِى السَّمَآءِ وَهُوَ السَّمِيْعُ الْعَلِيْمُ ﴿3X﴾

In the name of Allah ﷻ, through whose name nothing in the heavens or earth can cause any harm. And He is the One who hears and knows everything.

(Abu Dawood, Vol. 2, Pg. 346)

Virtue

Whosoever recites these words three times in the morning will be protected from **sudden calamities** until the night and whosoever recites these words three times in the evening will be protected from **sudden calamities** until the morning.

سُبْحَانَ اللهِ وَبِحَمْدِهٖ عَدَدَ خَلْقِهٖ وَرِضٰى نَفْسِهٖ وَزِنَةَ عَرْشِهٖ وَمِدَادَ كَلِمَاتِهٖ

I declare the purity of Allah Ta'ala together with His praises in numbers equivalent to His creatures in a manner befitting His pleasure in weight equal to His throne and in quantities equal to the ink of His words.

اَلصَّبَاحُ: اَللّٰهُمَّ مَا أَصْبَحَ بِيْ مِنْ نِعْمَةٍ أَوْ بِأَحَدٍ مِنْ خَلْقِكَ فَمِنْكَ وَحْدَكَ لَا شَرِيْكَ لَكَ فَلَكَ الْحَمْدُ وَلَكَ الشُّكْرُ

اَلْمَسَاءُ: اَللّٰهُمَّ مَا أَمْسٰى بِيْ مِنْ نِعْمَةٍ أَوْ بِأَحَدٍ مِّنْ خَلْقِكَ فَمِنْكَ وَحْدَكَ لَا شَرِيْكَ لَكَ فَلَكَ الْحَمْدُ وَلَكَ الشُّكْرُ ﴿3X﴾

O Allah! whatsoever blessing I or anyone of Your creation may find this morning / evening they are all from You; You are one and alone; You have no partner, so for You alone is all praise and all gratitude.

(Amal-ul-yaum-wal-laylah Ibne Sunni (R.A), Pg. 25)

58	Morning and Evening dua

$$اَللّٰهُمَّ بِكَ اَصْبَحْنَا وَبِكَ اَمْسَيْنَا وَبِكَ نَحْيٰى وَبِكَ نَمُوْتُ وَاِلَيْكَ النُّشُوْرُ$$

O Allah! with Your help do I start this day or night and with Your help do I live and with Your help do I die and to You is our rising.

(Abu Dawood Vol. 2 Pg. 343)

| 59 | Dua for protection from calamities |

Recite three times morning and evening

بِسْمِ اللهِ عَلٰى دِيْنِيْ وَنَفْسِيْ وَوَلَدِيْ وَاَهْلِيْ وَمَالِيْ

In the name of Allah ﷺ, (I seek protection) upon my religion, life, children, family and wealth.

(Kanzul Ummal, Vol. 2, Pg. 141)

Virtue

Hadhrat Ma'qal bin Yasaar R.A. narrates: "Once I expressed my fears to Rasulullah [PBUH] over five things in my life. I feared that I would be deviated from the Siraatul-Mustaqeem (straight path). The second was regarding my life. I feared harm or illness would befall me. The third was about my children that they would suffer Deeni or worldly harm. The fourth concern was my wife, that she too may suffer physical or spiritual harm. The fifth fear I had was over my wealth, should there occur a loss of income or property. After listening to my fears, Rasulullah ﷺ taught me the above dua.

(Kanzul-Ummaal, Vol. 2. Pg 636)

> حَسْبِيَ اللّٰهُ لَآ إِلٰهَ إِلَّا هُوَ عَلَيْهِ تَوَكَّلْتُ وَهُوَ رَبُّ الْعَرْشِ الْعَظِيمِ

Allah ﷾ is sufficient for me. There is none worthy of worship but He alone. On Him is my trust, He is the Rabb of the Supreme Throne.

60	Dua for protection on the day of Qiyaamah

(Recite three times after Fajar and Maghrib salaah)

رَضِيْتُ بِاللهِ رَبًّا وَّبِالْاِسْلَامِ دِيْنًا وَّبِمُحَمَّدٍ (صَلَّى اللهُ عَلَيْهِ وَسَلَّمَ) رَسُوْلًا وَّنَبِيًّا

I am happy with Allah ﷻ as my Rabb, with Islam as my religion and Muhammad [PBUH] as my prophet.

(Tirmizi, Vol. 2, Pg. 174)

Virtue

Whosoever recites these words in the morning or evening Allah ﷻ takes it upon Himself to please that person

| 61 | Dua for easy death |

$$\text{اَللّٰهُمَّ بَارِكْ لِيْ فِي الْمَوْتِ وَفِيْمَا بَعْدَ الْمَوْتِ}$$

O Allah, bless me at the time of my death and what follows after death. (Read it twenty-five times daily).

www.ingramcontent.com/pod-product-compliance
Lightning Source LLC
LaVergne TN
LVHW012127070526
838202LV00056B/5897